is to be returned on or before the

Hans Ander...

KU-547-211

Level 2

Retold by Karen Holmes
Series Editors: Andy Hopkins and Jocelyn Potter

Pearson Education Limited
Edinburgh Gate, Harlow,
Essex CM20 2JE, England
and Associated Companies throughout the world.

ISBN 0 582 421128

This edition first published 2000

5 7 9 10 8 6 4

NEW EDITION

Copyright © Penguin Books Ltd 2000
Illustrations by Gwen Tourret (opening illustration by Alan Fraser)
Cover design by Bender Richardson White

Typeset by Pantek Arts Ltd, Maidstone, Kent
Set in 11/14pt Bembo
Printed in China
GCC/04

Published by Pearson Education Limited in association with
Penguin Books Ltd, both companies being subsidiaries of Pearson Plc

For a complete list of titles available in the Penguin Readers series, please write to your local
Pearson Education office or to: Penguin Readers Marketing Department,
Pearson Education, Edinburgh Gate, Harlow, Essex CM20 2JE.

Contents

Introduction

The duckling was very unhappy. 'They don't like me because I'm ugly,' he thought.

Nobody spoke to him or went near him. His brothers and sisters were unkind, too. 'We want the cat to catch you, you ugly duckling!' they cried.

Hans Andersen wrote about animals – but his animals can talk! He also wrote about children and little people. Some animals and people in his stories are very good and some are very bad. Sometimes his stories are happy – but at times they are very sad.

In this book, you will read about an ugly duckling with no friends. Will he always be unhappy? The second story is about a nightingale, a little bird. She lives in a lovely wood, but then a king hears about her beautiful songs. In the third story, a mermaid loves a handsome prince and wants to live with him on land. The fourth story is about an emperor's very strange new clothes. And the last story is about a very small girl, Thumbelina. Who will love her? And who will she love?

Hans Christian Andersen was born in Denmark in 1805. His father made shoes and his mother could not read or write. He went to school and university in Copenhagen.

After he left university, he wrote a lot of stories. Many people in Europe liked them. But today children all over the world love the stories of Hans Andersen.

Animals in these Stories

duck

duckling

hen

geese

swan

nightingale

cow

toad

beetle

field mouse

mole

The Ugly Duckling

A duck sat on her eggs in the woods. She sat there for a long time. Then the eggs opened and some ducklings came out.

The ducklings put their heads outside the eggs. 'Tchick, tchick!' they said.

'Quack, quack!' answered the mother duck. She stood up. 'They aren't all here,' she thought. 'The largest egg isn't open. Do I have to sit here all day?' She sat down again.

An hour later, the big egg opened. 'Tchick, tchick,' said the duckling, and it fell out of the egg. But oh! It was very big and ugly! The duck looked at it. 'That's a very big duckling!' she said. 'It's very strange.'

◆

The next day the mother duck took the ducklings down to the river. She jumped into the water. 'Quack, quack!' she cried, and the ducklings jumped into the water too. The water went over their heads, but the ducklings started to swim. The ugly duckling jumped in the water, too.

'He can swim. He's a clever duckling,' the mother duck thought. 'He's quite pretty now, in the water.' She called to her ducklings: 'Quack, quack! Come with me! We're going to see the other ducks. But stay near me – and don't go near the cat!'

So they went into the garden, and the ducklings stayed near their mother. But the other ducks looked at them and said, 'Now there are too many ducks in this garden. And that big duckling is very ugly. We don't want him here.'

One of the ducks started to push him away.

'Leave him,' the mother duck said. 'He won't hurt you.'

'He's big and ugly, so we don't want him near us,' the ducks said.

An hour later, the big egg opened.

'He isn't beautiful, but he's a very good child,' the mother duck told the other ducks. 'He's clever and he swims very well. He stayed in his egg for a long time, so he's different from the other ducklings.'

But the ducks and hens were unkind to the poor duckling. 'He's so big!' they all said.

The duckling was very unhappy. 'They don't like me because I'm ugly,' he thought.

Nobody spoke to him or went near him. His brothers and sisters were unkind, too. 'We want the cat to catch you, you ugly duckling!' they cried.

After the first day, the mother duck said sadly, 'I want you to go away!'

The ugly duckling ran out of the garden. The little birds in the trees were afraid. 'They're afraid of me because I'm ugly,' the duckling thought.

He ran and ran. Then he came to a big field. Some wild ducks lived there. He stayed in the field all night.

In the morning the wild ducks saw the duckling. 'Who are you?' they asked. The ugly duckling could not answer. Poor thing! He was very sad.

He stayed in the field for two days. Then two wild geese talked to him. 'You're very ugly but we like you,' they said kindly. 'Come with us and be a wild bird.'

◆

BANG! It was the sound of a gun. The two wild geese fell down dead on the ground. BANG! A lot of wild geese flew up into the sky. BANG!

There were men with guns everywhere. First they killed the wild geese. Then their dogs ran through the fields to the river. The duckling was afraid and closed his eyes.

A big dog came near him. When he saw the duckling, he

opened his big mouth. Then he looked at the duckling again and ran away.

'The dog doesn't want to eat me because I'm ugly!' the duckling thought.

All day he heard the sound of the guns. He waited a long time before he left the river. Then he ran very quickly across the fields.

◆

The duckling came to a small house. The door of the house was open, so he walked inside.

An old woman lived in the house with her cat and her hen. The next morning the cat and the hen saw the duckling and made a lot of noise.

'What is it?' the old woman asked. She looked everywhere in the room, but her eyes were not good.

'Oh, it's a fat duck!' she said. 'Good! Now I'll have duck's eggs.'

The old woman, the cat and the hen watched the duckling. They waited for a long time, but there were no eggs. The cat and the hen got angry with the duckling.

'Where are your eggs?' the hen asked.

'I haven't got any eggs,' the duckling answered.

'Then don't talk to us.'

And the cat said, 'Can you make a nice noise? *I* make a nice noise – purr, purr.'

'No, I can't,' the duckling answered.

'Then don't talk to us,' the cat said.

The poor duckling was very unhappy. 'I want to go into the river again,' he told the hen.

'Why?' the hen asked. 'You're only thinking about the river because you're bored. Give us some eggs! Then you'll be busy and you won't think about the river.'

'But it's nice in the river,' the duckling said. 'The water goes over your head. It's very nice.'

'You're ill!' the hen said. 'Ask the cat. She thinks you're ill too! Who wants water over their head? Nobody! Ask the old woman. She'll tell you. *She* doesn't want to go in the river!'

'But it's very nice,' the duckling said again.

'What? Nice? Do you know more than the cat and the old woman? You live in a nice house with kind people. Be happy! Give them some eggs, or make nice noises.'

'I want to go to the fields and the woods and the river again,' the duckling said.

'Then go now,' said the hen.

◆

So the duckling went to the river and jumped into the water. But nobody spoke to him because he was so ugly.

It was winter. The days were very cold and it started to snow. 'I'm going to die,' the poor duckling thought.

One night, when it was nearly dark, some large, white birds flew near him. 'They're very beautiful birds,' he thought. They were swans. They flew up and up in the sky. They were on their way to a warm country across the sea. The ugly duckling watched them for a long time.

'Ah! I'll always remember those beautiful birds. What are they? Where are they going?' he thought. He loved them more than anything. 'I don't want to be as beautiful as those birds. I know that isn't possible. But why can't I live with the other ducks in the garden? Then I'll be happy.'

The river was so cold! The duckling could not stay in the water because it was too cold. One night, he fell down in the snow.

In the morning a man came to the river. He saw the duckling and he took the little bird home to his wife.

The man's children wanted to play with him, but the duckling was afraid. When he tried to run away, he fell into some milk. The man's wife shouted, and the duckling was more afraid. He jumped onto some food and ran everywhere.

The woman shouted again and hit him. The children tried to catch him and they shouted, too. The door was open, so the duckling ran out into the snow.

The poor duckling walked through the fields and the woods. Sometimes he wanted to sit down in the snow and die. But he lived through the winter and one day he saw the sun again.

◆

The duckling stood up. He was bigger now and he could fly high up in the sky. Up, up he flew!

He came down in a large garden by a river. There were a lot of beautiful trees in the garden. Oh! Everything was lovely!

Three beautiful white swans flew down from the sky to the river and sat on the water. The duckling remembered them. 'I saw those birds before,' he thought. 'I'll go and talk to them. They'll kill me because I'm ugly. But I'll try.'

He ran to the water and swam to the beautiful birds.

'Kill me,' said the poor duckling. He put his head down near the water, and he saw . . . What did he see in the water? He saw a swan! He was not a fat, ugly duckling, he was a swan! He was born from a swan's egg!

The other swans were happy to see him. Then some little children ran into the garden. They threw bread into the water, and the youngest child cried, 'There's a new swan!'

The other children looked at him. 'The new bird's very young and beautiful,' they said. 'He's the most beautiful swan in the world!'

The young swan was very happy! 'Nobody liked me before,' he thought, 'but now I'm beautiful. And I'm the happiest swan in the world!'

The Nightingale

A king lived in a beautiful palace. The palace had a very big garden with a lot of lovely flowers. People walked through the garden and looked at the flowers. Then they walked through a beautiful wood to the sea.

A nightingale lived in a tree in the wood. It sang beautifully! Every night an old man came through the wood to the sea. He wanted to catch fish. He stood and listened to the little bird. 'Oh, that's a pretty song!' he thought, and he cried.

Visitors from many other countries came to see the king. 'We like your city, your palace and your garden,' they told the king. 'They're very beautiful.'

Some visitors heard the little bird. 'Nothing is as beautiful as the nightingale's voice,' they said. They wrote books about the city, the palace and the garden, and they always wrote wonderful things about the nightingale.

Other people round the world read these books, and one day the king saw one. He read and read and he was very happy. 'But nothing is as good as the nightingale's voice,' the book said.

'What's this?' asked the king. 'The nightingale? I don't know this bird! Is there really a bird with a beautiful voice in my garden? Nobody told me. We learn a lot of new things from books.'

So the king called his most important servant.

'People say there's a very pretty bird here,' said the king. 'They say that it sings very beautifully. I want the nightingale to sing to me tonight.'

'I don't know this nightingale,' said the servant, 'but I'll find it.'

But where was the bird? The servant ran everywhere. He asked the other servants, but they knew nothing about it. He went to the king and said, 'There's no nightingale here. I can't find it.'

'A great king sent me this book,' said the king. 'It says there's a nightingale in my garden. Bring it here now or I'll be very angry.'

The servant ran through the palace and its gardens, and the other servants ran, too. Then they found a young girl in the palace kitchen and asked her about the nightingale.

'Oh, yes! It sings in the wood near the sea. It has a beautiful voice! I take some food through the wood to my mother every night because she's very ill. Sometimes I sit down in the wood and then I hear the nightingale's song.'

'Little girl,' said the servant, 'please take us to the nightingale.'

The other servants went with them. On their way to the wood, they heard a cow. 'There's the nightingale,' one man said. 'It sings very nicely.'

'No, that's a cow,' the little girl said. 'We're a long way from the nightingale's home.'

Near a small river in the garden some toads started to make a noise.

'Now I can hear it,' said a servant.

'No, those are toads. They have ugly voices!' said the little girl. 'But we'll hear the nightingale in these trees.'

Then the small bird started to sing. 'There it is!' the little girl said. She showed them a little bird in one of the trees.

'Is that the nightingale?' asked a servant. 'It isn't very pretty. The other birds are prettier and more interesting.'

'Little nightingale!' the girl called. 'Our king wants you to sing something to him.'

'I'll be happy to sing to the king,' the nightingale said.

'It has a beautiful voice,' said the servant. 'It will make the king and his friends very happy.'

'Where is the king?' the little bird asked. 'Isn't he here in the wood?'

'Pretty little bird, you're going to the king's palace tonight. You'll sing there,' the servant said.

'I live happily in the green trees. Can I sing inside a palace? I don't know,' said the nightingale. 'But the king wants me to sing to him so I'll try.' And the little bird went with the servants to the palace.

◆

The king sat in a great room in his palace, and the nightingale sat on a table. The king's servants and his friends were in the room. They all looked at the nightingale.

The little bird started to sing. It sang beautifully. The king started to cry – and so everybody cried with him.

'Your songs make me happy,' the king said. 'I'll give you some pretty shoes.'

'Thank you,' the nightingale said, 'but I don't want anything. You cry when you hear my songs. And that makes *me* happy.' Then it sang again.

'Please stay in my palace,' said the king. 'You can go out into the wood every morning and afternoon, and again every night.'

He gave the nightingale servants. They went everywhere with the little bird.

◆

One day somebody brought a box to the king. It was another nightingale, but it was wood.

'What's this?' the king asked. 'It can't eat or drink. It can't walk or run. But can it sing?' He looked at his servants. 'Let's hear it!'

Somebody turned the key. The nightingale could only sing one song, but it sang this song many times.

Then the king said, 'I want to hear *my* nightingale sing. Where is it?'

'It flew out of the open window to its home in the wood,' a servant said.

'It flew away? Why?' the king asked.

'That old nightingale isn't as good as this new bird,' the king's friends said. 'This nightingale will sing all day.'

The people in the city came and listened to the new bird. Its song made them very happy. But the old man from the wood said, 'The new nightingale has a pretty voice, but the little nightingale's voice is better.'

◆

The servants put the new nightingale on a table near the king's bed. People wrote long books about the new nightingale. Not many people could read these long books. But they liked them because the king did.

The new nightingale sang for a year. The king, his friends, and the people in the city knew its song; it always sang the same song in the same way. So now people could sing with the nightingale. The little boys in the street sang the nightingale's song. The king sang its song, too.

'You sing beautifully,' the servants told him.

But one night there was a noise inside the nightingale. Bang! Now the bird could not sing.

The king jumped quickly out of bed, and called for help. 'Why can't the nightingale sing?' he asked. 'Look inside it.'

A man opened the nightingale and looked inside it. Then he turned the key, and it sang again. But he said, 'This bird can't sing every day now. It can only sing for one day every year.'

◆

Five years later, the king was very ill. People said, 'He isn't going to live. There will be a new king.'

The king looked cold and white in his beautiful bed. 'He's dead,' his friends thought. They went away and visited the new king.

But the king was not dead. A window was open near his bed, and the king looked out at the beautiful sky.

'I'm going to die,' he thought. 'I did many good things in my life... and many bad things, too. I don't want to think about those things.'

He called to the nightingale on the table, 'Sing, little nightingale, please, please, sing!' But the nightingale did not sing.

Then the king heard a sound outside – a beautiful voice. The nightingale from the wood sat on a tree and sang. It sang about beautiful flowers, and woods and gardens.

The king was happy again. 'Thank you, thank you,' he said to the bird. 'You beautiful little bird, you came back and helped me. I won't die now. What can I give you?'

'You gave me something very beautiful when I first sang for you,' the nightingale said. 'You cried. I will always remember that day. But I'll sing now, and you sleep.'

The nightingale sang and the king slept. Later he opened his eyes and saw the sun in the sky.

'Where are my servants?' he asked. 'They aren't in the palace. Do they think I'm dead? Are they with the new king?'

The little nightingale sat next to him and sang.

'Please stay with me,' the king said. 'I'll throw the other bird away.'

'Don't throw the other bird away,' said the nightingale. 'It wanted to make you happy, but it couldn't sing every day. I can't stay inside your palace because my home is in the woods. But I'll come here sometimes. I'll sit in this tree near your window and I'll sing for you.'

Then the nightingale flew away.

The servants came into the room and looked at the dead king. But he was not dead! The king sat up. 'Good morning!' he said.

The nightingale from the wood sat on a tree and sang.

The Little Mermaid

In the middle of the sea the water is very, very blue. You can see through it. Below the water is a strange world of beautiful trees and plants. Fish swim in and out of them. This is the home of the Sea King. His palace is here, under the water.

After the Sea King's wife died, his old mother looked after him. She loved the Sea King's six children, and they loved their grandmother, too. These children were beautiful mermaid princesses. The youngest princess was the most beautiful: her eyes were as blue as the sea and her face was as white as snow. But mermaids do not have feet. The top half of her body was the body of a girl, and the bottom half was the body of a fish.

Sometimes the old grandmother told stories to the mermaid princesses. 'There are many people in the world,' she said. 'Some people live in the sea and some live on the land. The land people are different. They have feet.'

'Tell me everything,' the youngest mermaid said.

'These people are men,' her grandmother said. 'They have ships and they have great cities. There are mountains and gardens with beautiful flowers. Fish fly through the sky and sing beautiful songs!' (These 'fish' were birds, but she called them fish. The little princesses did not know about birds.)

'On your fifteenth birthday, you can swim to the top of the sea,' their grandmother said. 'You can sit there at night and see the ships. And you can learn about men.'

The youngest sister wanted to swim to the top of the sea more than the other sisters. On many nights she stood by the open window, and looked up through the blue water. She saw a ship above her. 'That's a very big fish,' she thought.

◆

The next year, the oldest sister was fifteen and she swam to the top of the sea. She came back and said to her sisters, 'I saw many things. I saw a lovely big city. It was near the sea and there were a lot of lights. People sang and talked. I wanted to go there but I stayed in the sea.'

'Tell me about the city again,' the youngest princess said. The next night she stood near her open window and looked up through the sea. 'I can hear singing,' she thought.

The next year another sister was fifteen and she went to the top of the sea. The next day she came home.

'It was very beautiful,' she told her sisters. 'The sky, the land — it's the most beautiful place in the world.'

Then the third sister was fifteen and she went to the top of the sea. She was not afraid of anything, and she swam up a river. She saw mountains and woods and houses. 'The birds sang and children jumped into the water. Then a little dog ran after me and I was afraid. I left the river and came back to the sea. I'll always remember the lovely woods, the houses and the pretty children,' she said.

The next sister went, but she stayed in the sea. She came back home and said to her sisters, 'I saw ships on the water. They were as beautiful as big white birds.'

The next year, another sister was fifteen. But it was winter and there was snow everywhere on the land. She was cold and came back home very quickly.

The five sisters were very happy. They sometimes went to look at ships, cities and men. But they came home and forgot these things. 'Our home is more beautiful than anything above the water,' they said. When the weather was bad, they went up again, hand in hand. They swam in front of the ships and sang to the people on them.

'We live under the sea and we're very happy! Don't be afraid. Come down to us,' they sang.

The youngest princess had to stay in her father's palace. She wanted to cry, but mermaids cannot cry.

'Oh, I want to be fifteen!' she thought. 'I want to see the land and the people. I want to swim to the top of the sea!'

◆

One day her grandmother said, 'Today is your fifteenth birthday. Now you can go to the top of the sea.'

The little mermaid swam up above the water that night. She saw a big ship on the sea, and there were hundreds of lights on the ship. She looked through the windows and saw a lot of men in rich clothes. The most beautiful man was a young prince with big blue eyes.

'I want to stay here,' the little mermaid thought. 'I want to look at this beautiful prince.'

But there was a strong wind, and the sea was suddenly dangerous. Water went into the big ship.

The little mermaid liked the bad weather, but the people on the ship were afraid. Suddenly the ship broke into two halves and it started to go down.

'Now the prince can come to my city in the sea,' the little mermaid thought. 'I want him to visit my palace. But can men live in water? He'll die! I don't want him to die!'

She swam quickly to the prince and put her hands under his head. His head was above the water, but he did not open his eyes.

Morning came, and the little mermaid touched the prince's face. 'Don't die!' she cried. She looked at the land. It was winter and there was a lot of snow on the mountains. There was a wood near the sea, and a big church in the wood. The little mermaid swam to the land with the prince. She left him near the church, then she went back to the sea.

A young girl came out of the church. She saw the prince and was afraid. 'Is he dead?' she thought.

The most beautiful man was a young prince with big blue eyes.

She called other people from the church and they helped the prince. From the sea, the little mermaid saw the prince open his eyes. He was not dead!

'What happened?' the prince asked. 'I can't remember anything.' They took him into the church.

The little mermaid was very sad. 'He doesn't remember me,' she thought. She swam back to her father's palace under the sea.

'What did you see?' her sisters asked her, but the little mermaid did not answer.

She often went back to the church and looked for the young prince. Now it was spring. There was no snow on the mountains and there were flowers in the woods. But she never saw the prince.

Then she told her story to one of her sisters. 'I'm sad because I love the prince,' she said.

The sister told the story to the other princesses and they told their friends. One friend knew about the prince. 'He lives in a palace near the sea,' she said.

'Come, little sister!' said the princesses. And the six mermaids swam to the top of the water in front of the prince's palace.

◆

It was a great white palace with beautiful rooms. 'This is the home of my prince,' the little mermaid thought.

She went there every night. She looked in at the young prince through the windows, and she listened to his servants. 'The prince is a good man,' they said.

She liked the people on the land. 'I want to live here,' she thought. 'I want to go on a ship. I want to walk in the gardens and woods.'

'I want to know everything about the land people,' she said to her sisters.

'We don't know anything about them,' her sisters said. 'Ask grandmother.'

'Do men live for a long time?' she asked her grandmother.

'No, they die. Their lives are shorter than ours. We live for 300 years, then we change into sea water. We never live again. Land people have souls. Their bodies die, but their souls go to a beautiful place in the sky. Then they're very happy.'

'I don't want to live for 300 years,' the little mermaid said. 'I want to be a land person. I want a soul. I want my soul to go to that beautiful place in the sky. Tell me, how can I get a soul?'

'Sometimes a man loves somebody more than he loves his father and mother,' her grandmother answered. 'He marries her and she can stay with him. Then she gets a soul. But you can't live on the land! The people on the land are afraid of mermaids. And you can't walk without feet!'

The little princess looked sadly down at her body. 'I'm beautiful,' she thought, 'as beautiful as the people on the land. But I haven't got any feet. A friend told me about an old woman. She knows about magic, so perhaps she can help me.'

◆

There were a lot of ugly plants with long arms near the old woman's house. There were dead people in their arms, and the little mermaid was afraid. But she remembered the prince and swam past them. She found the old woman.

'What do you want?' the old woman said. 'You want to have two feet and live on the land? You want the prince to love you and give you a soul? I can help you, but you'll be very unhappy. Here's a magic drink. Take it to the land, then drink it. You'll have feet, but they'll hurt. Do you understand? Do you really want to be a land person? You can never be a mermaid again.'

'I do want to be a land person,' the mermaid answered. She wanted her prince and she wanted a soul.

'Then marry your prince, or you'll die,' the old woman said. 'You can't go back to your sisters. You'll change into seawater. And there is one more thing. On the land, you won't speak or sing.'

'But how will the prince love me then?' the princess asked.

'The prince will love your beautiful face. And you can speak to him with your eyes,' the old woman answered. 'He'll love you. Do you want the magic drink?'

'Yes,' said the little mermaid.

◆

She swam to the prince's palace and drank the magic drink. Her legs, her arms, her head . . . everything started to hurt. She fell down and slept. When she opened her eyes again, the beautiful prince was there.

'Who are you? Where do you come from?' the prince asked her. She looked at him with her blue eyes, but she could not speak. The prince took her into the palace. She walked beautifully and everybody looked at her. But her feet hurt and she wanted to cry.

At the prince's palace, he gave her lovely clothes. She was beautiful. But she could not speak or sing. This made her sad. 'I want the prince to hear my beautiful songs,' she thought.

The little mermaid walked through the woods with her prince. She went to the mountains and to beautiful gardens with him. Her feet hurt, but she could not speak. And she could not cry. At night she went down to the sea near the prince's palace and put her feet in the cold water. 'Where are my sisters?' she thought.

One night, she sat with her feet in the water, and her sisters came. 'Everybody in our father's palace is sad because you left us,' they told her.

Every night after that the five sisters came. One night they brought their old grandmother. One night they brought their father, the great Sea King. But these two old people could not swim near the land so they could not speak to the little princess.

◆

The young prince loved the little mermaid. 'You are very beautiful,' he said.

The little mermaid was afraid. 'He loves me but will he marry me? I have to marry him. I don't want to die!' she thought. 'Do you love me?' her eyes asked the prince. He kissed her.

'Yes, I love you,' said the prince. 'You're a good, kind child, and you love me. But I can't marry you. I was on a ship one day and the ship went down. The sea threw me onto the land near a church. A girl came out of the church and helped me. I only saw her for one day, but I want to marry her.'

'He doesn't remember me,' the little mermaid thought sadly.

◆

'I'm going to visit a beautiful princess,' the prince said to the little mermaid one day. 'My father and mother want me to see her. But I won't marry her − I don't love her. You're my best friend. Come with me on the ship.'

He kissed her on her mouth and took her in his arms. The little mermaid was very happy.

At night, on the ship, everybody was asleep. The little mermaid sat and looked down into the sea. She saw her sisters. They looked sad. 'I'm very happy,' she thought, 'but I can't tell my sisters that. I can't speak.'

The next morning the ship came to a great city, and they went to see the princess.

'She's the girl from the church!' the prince cried. 'I want to marry her.' And he kissed the princess's hand.

The little mermaid looked at him sadly. 'He'll marry the princess,' she thought, 'and then I'll die.'

◆

So the prince married his princess. The little mermaid stood near them and watched. But she saw and heard nothing. 'Now he can never marry me,' she thought. 'Now I'm really going to die.'

That night, the prince and the princess went onto the ship. There were lights everywhere, and everybody was very happy. But the poor little mermaid was sad.

'I left my home. I can't speak and sing. My legs hurt, and the prince will never be my husband,' she thought. 'I have to die now, so this is my last night.'

When everybody was asleep, her sisters came out of the sea. 'We went to the old woman,' they told her. 'Kill the prince before tomorrow morning, then you won't die. You'll lose your feet and you'll be a mermaid again. But be quick! We're waiting for you.' They swam away.

The little mermaid went into the prince's room. He was asleep. 'No!' she thought. 'I love him! I can't kill him.' She kissed him and left.

'I'll die,' she thought. Then she jumped into the sea. She saw the ship and the sky above her. Then she heard a sound. There were people in the sky! She looked at her body. She was not a mermaid – her body was the same as the people in the sky! She flew up and up into the sky.

'Who are you?' she asked people.

'We're the children of the sky,' was the answer. 'We aren't land people or sea people. We help other people. We bring rain and flowers to dry lands. We make sad people happy. We do good things for 300 years, and then we go to a great and beautiful country in the sky. You, little mermaid, are also a good person. You helped the prince. Now you can make other people happy. Now you are a sky person.'

The little mermaid looked down at the ship. She saw the prince with his pretty young wife. They looked sadly down at the sea. Where was she? Was she in the sea? She went down near to the prince but he could not see her.

'I'll do good things for 300 years,' she thought. 'Then I can stay in that beautiful place up in the sky and I will always be happy.'

'Sometimes it isn't 300 years,' said a sky sister. 'We go into children's houses. Nobody can see us, but we're there. Sometimes we find a bad child, and then we stay here for another year. But one day we'll live in that beautiful place in the sky.'

The Emperor's New Clothes

This is a story about an emperor. He loved new clothes, and he had different clothes for every hour of the day.

One day two men visited him. They liked money, but they did not want to work for it.

'We can make wonderful cloth,' they said. 'It's very beautiful cloth, so only clever people can see it.'

'I like it,' the emperor thought. 'Make this cloth – then make me some clothes,' he said to the men. 'Some people won't see them, but they're stupid people!' He gave a lot of money to the two men.

Every day the men asked the king for more money. 'We're working hard,' they said. But they did not make any cloth.

◆

The emperor waited and waited. He wanted his new cloth, but he did not want to visit the two men. And he was afraid. 'Perhaps I won't see the cloth,' he thought. 'Then everybody will know that I'm not a clever man.'

He called a servant. 'Go and look at the new cloth. Ask them: "When will it be ready?"'

The servant went to the men's house, but what did he see? Nothing! There was no cloth. 'What are they doing?' the servant thought.

'Come nearer,' one of the men said. 'Do you like our cloth? Isn't it beautiful?'

The servant looked and looked, but he saw nothing. 'I don't understand,' he thought. 'Am I stupid? I can't tell anybody about this.' He spoke to the men: 'Oh, it's very good – very good,' he said. 'The cloth is beautiful. I'll tell the emperor.'

The emperor waited for two more weeks, then he called another servant. 'When will the cloth be ready?' he cried. 'Find those two men. Ask them!'

This servant went to the two men. They showed him the cloth, but he couldn't see anything.

'Isn't the cloth beautiful?' one of the bad men said. 'The other servant liked it.'

The man thought, 'I can't see the cloth! I'm stupid! But I don't want anybody to know.' He went back to the emperor and said, 'The cloth is wonderful!'

After two or three days, the people in the city started to talk about the beautiful cloth. 'It's very beautiful, but stupid people can't see it,' they said.

◆

Now the emperor really wanted to see the cloth. He took his servants with him and went to the men's house.

'Isn't the cloth beautiful?' said the two men. 'Please look at it. Isn't it pretty? Touch it.' And they put out their hands and showed him.

'I can see nothing,' the emperor thought. 'This is very, very bad. Am I stupid? A stupid man can't be emperor.'

He looked at the men's hands and said to his servants, 'Oh, the cloth is beautiful. I like it.'

The servants looked and looked. But they saw nothing. 'Beautiful! Lovely! Very pretty!' they said. 'The men will make some clothes from this cloth now.'

The emperor happily gave the two men more money.

That night the two men did not go to bed. There were lights in every room in the house.

'The emperor and his people think we're working,' they thought.

'Oh, the cloth is beautiful. I like it.'

Next morning, they went to the palace. 'The emperor's new clothes are ready,' they cried.

◆

The emperor went to their house with his servants. The two bad men put out their arms.

'Here are your clothes,' the men said. 'Put them on.'

'Yes, yes!' said the servants. But they could not see the clothes.

The emperor took off his old shirt and trousers. The two men walked round him and touched his arms and legs.

'We can't see any clothes,' the servants thought. But they said nothing.

'You look wonderful in your new clothes!' everybody cried. 'They are clothes for an emperor!'

'I am ready now. I will walk through the streets,' the emperor said. He looked at his arms and legs. 'These new clothes feel very good. They aren't too big or too small.'

He walked through the streets with his servants and the great men of the country. People stood outside their houses or looked out of the windows. 'Oh, our emperor's new clothes are very beautiful!' they cried. But they thought: 'We can't see any clothes. Are we stupid?'

Then a little child spoke: 'The emperor has no clothes!'

'Be quiet!' his father said. But it was too late.

'The emperor has no clothes!' a man near the child repeated to the woman next to him. She told her friend: 'The emperor has no clothes!'

'The emperor has no clothes!' the people cried. And they started to laugh.

The emperor was angry. 'The people are right,' he thought. 'But I have to walk through the streets.' He walked and walked. His servants and great men followed him, but they knew too. The emperor had no clothes!

Thumbelina

A woman wanted a baby. 'How can I get a child?' she thought. 'I know. I'll go and see the old woman. She knows about magic. She can help me.'

She went to the old woman's house. 'I want a baby,' she said. 'Tell me, where can I get a child?'

'Oh, that's very easy,' the old woman said. 'Here's a magic flower. Plant it in a small box and wait.'

The woman went home with the magic flower and put it in a box. The next day there was another beautiful large flower in the box.

'This is a beautiful flower!' said the woman, and she kissed it. She kissed it again and the flower opened. There was a baby girl inside the flower. She was a lovely little girl, but she was very, very small!

'She's very small,' the woman said. 'I'll call her Thumbelina.'

Thumbelina lived inside her flower on the woman's table.

◆

One night, Thumbelina was asleep in her flower when an old toad came through the window. The toad was very big and very ugly. She jumped onto the table next to Thumbelina.

'Thumbelina is very beautiful. I want her to marry my son,' thought the toad. She took the flower and Thumbelina and she jumped through the window and down into the garden.

The toad lived with her son in a field near a river. Ugh! Her son was very ugly!

He saw the beautiful little girl in the flower. 'Croak! Croak! Brek-kek-kek!' he said.

'Don't speak,' said the old toad. 'She'll wake up and run away.

There was a baby girl inside the flower.

We'll put her in the river in this flower. Then she can't get away.'

The next morning, Thumbelina opened her eyes. She was on a big river and she was afraid. Where was the land? Where was her home?

The old toad and her ugly son swam to Thumbelina. 'You'll be his wife,' the old toad said. 'You'll live in a field near the river.'

'Croak! Croak! Brek-kek-kek!' her son said.

Little Thumbelina cried and cried. She did not want to live in the ugly toad's house. The little fish in the river heard her. They swam to her and looked at her sadly. Then they pushed the flower and it moved down the river.

The little flower started to move quickly. The toads were too slow and could not follow the flower.

The little birds in the trees saw Thumbelina. 'She's a lovely little girl!' they said. And the flower moved away down the river.

A big beetle saw Thumbelina on her flower. He caught her and took her up into a tree. Then he sat with her in the tree and gave her a flower. 'Eat this,' he said. 'I like you. You're not a beetle but you're very pretty.'

The other beetles wanted to look at little Thumbelina. 'She's only got two legs!' they said. 'She's very ugly! Is she a little girl? Girls are very ugly.'

The big beetle looked at Thumbelina again. 'My friends think she's ugly,' he thought. 'She *is* ugly!'

He took her down from the tree and put her on a flower. Poor Thumbelina cried and cried. 'Nobody likes me,' she thought. 'They all think I'm ugly.'

◆

Poor Thumbelina lived in the great wood for a long time. She had no friends, and she slept under a flower. It was winter and the days were very cold. The birds started to fly away and the flowers began to die. Then it started to snow.

There was a big field near the wood. Thumbelina walked into the field and she came to a very small house. It was the home of a field mouse. Thumbelina stood at the door.

'Poor little girl,' said the field mouse. 'You're sad and cold. Come into my house and eat some food.'

The field mouse liked Thumbelina. 'You can stay with me through the winter,' she said. 'But I want you to tell me stories. I like stories.'

Every day Thumbelina told the field mouse a different story.

Then one day the field mouse said, 'My friend's coming to my house. He's very rich and he's got a big house. Marry him and you'll be very happy.'

But Thumbelina did not want to marry the mouse's friend. Her friend was a mole.

'He's very rich and very clever,' said the field mouse. 'But he doesn't like the sun. He lives under the ground. He never sees the beautiful flowers.'

The mole came to the house and saw Thumbelina. He wanted her to sing for him. He heard her singing and he liked her. But he said nothing; he was a very quiet mole.

◆

The mole made a little road from his house, deep under the ground, to the field mouse's house.

One day Thumbelina, the field mouse and the mole walked down this road. Thumbelina saw a bird near the mole's house.

'That bird died because he was cold,' Thumbelina said. She was very sad. She loved little birds.

'Who wants to be a bird?' the mole asked. 'A bird says "tweet-tweet" all day and flies up in the sky. But in winter it's very cold. Then the birds die.'

Thumbelina said nothing. The field mouse and the mole walked down the road, but she stayed with the bird. She kissed it.

That night Thumbelina could not sleep. She got out of her bed and took some flowers to the bird. She made a bed from the flowers. 'I'll make him warm,' she thought. Then she sat down next to him. But the bird was not dead! He opened his eyes.

The next night she went to the bird again. He was not dead, but he was very ill. He opened his eyes again and looked at Thumbelina.

'Thank you, pretty little child,' the bird said. 'I'm warmer now. Tomorrow I'll get up and fly into the sky again.'

Thumbelina said, 'Don't go – it's very cold. There's snow everywhere. Stay in your bed. I'll bring you food and water.'

The bird stayed there for days, and Thumbelina brought him water in a flower and some food. She did not tell the field mouse and the mole about the bird.

One day it was warmer. The sun came out and the bird got up.

'Look at the beautiful sun,' he said to Thumbelina. 'Come away with me. You can sit on my back.'

'No, I can't!' Thumbelina said. 'The mouse wants me to stay here.'

'Then goodbye, goodbye, you good, pretty girl!' said the bird. He flew up and up into the sky. Thumbelina watched him. She liked the little bird; he was her friend. She started to cry.

'Tweet-tweet! Tweet-tweet!' the bird sang, and flew up and up. Thumbelina could not see him now.

◆

'You're going to marry the mole, Thumbelina,' said the field mouse. 'He wants you to be his wife. You'll be very happy! Start work and make some beautiful clothes.'

Thumbelina worked hard. Every night the mole visited her. 'Next month it will be cooler. Then I'll marry you,' he said.

Every morning Thumbelina went outside and looked at the sun. 'It's beautiful,' she thought. 'I don't want to live under the ground. I'll never see the sun again. And I want to see my friend, the little bird.'

'I can't marry the mole,' she told the field mouse.

'You *will* marry him,' said the field mouse. 'Marry him or I'll hurt you with my white teeth.'

One day the mole came to the field mouse's house. 'Today you're going to marry me,' he said.

Poor little Thumbelina was very sad. She went for a walk. 'Goodbye, sun,' she said. Then she heard a wonderful sound.

'Tweet-tweet! Tweet-tweet!' Her friend, the bird, came down out of the sky.

'I don't want to marry the ugly mole,' Thumbelina cried. 'And I don't want to live under the ground. I want to see the sun.'

'It's nearly winter. The days will be cold again,' the bird said. 'I'm going away to a warm country. Come with me! You can sit on my back. We'll go away from the ugly mole – over the mountains, to a wonderful country with lovely flowers.'

'Yes, I'll come with you!' Thumbelina said, and climbed onto the bird's back. Then the bird and Thumbelina flew up into the sky over woods, across the sea and over mountains.

They came to a warm country. It was never cold there and the sun looked bigger. There was fruit on the trees and there were lovely flowers. Happy children played in the gardens. They stopped at some big trees near a wide river.

'My home's in those trees,' the bird said. 'But *you* can't live in a tree. You'll have to live in a flower. Look at those beautiful flowers. Tell me, which flower do you like? I'll put you down on it.'

The bird flew down and put Thumbelina on a beautiful white flower. There was a little man inside it.

'A little man or woman lives in each flower,' he said. 'I'm the prince of the little people.'

'He's very beautiful!' said Thumbelina to the bird.

The little prince was afraid of the big bird. But he looked again at Thumbelina and he felt happy. She was very, very pretty.

'What's your name?' he asked her.

'Thumbelina,' she said.

'I want to marry you,' said the prince. 'I'll make you princess of the flowers.'

'Yes, yes,' cried Thumbelina.

A little man and a little lady, a little boy and a little girl came out of every flower. Everybody was happy.

'Thumbelina is an ugly name for a pretty girl,' the prince said. 'We'll call you Maia.'

So Maia and the prince lived happily with their friends in their beautiful country.

ACTIVITIES

The Ugly Duckling and The Nightingale

Before you read

1 Look at the pictures of animals at the beginning of the book. What do you know about ducks and nightingales? Where do they live?

2 Find these words in your dictionary. They are all in the story.

   field key king palace poor servant tale voice wild

   a Which are words for:
   - people?
   - places?
   - a story?

   b What do you:
   - speak with?
   - open a door with?

   c Use the other words in these sentences:
   - The ..... ducks fly to Canada in summer.
   - The ..... girl was very sad.

After you read

3 Answer the questions.

   a Why don't the other birds and animals in the story like the duckling?

   b What happens to the ugly duckling at the end of the story?

   c Why does the king like nightingales?

   d What happens to the second nightingale?

4 What lessons can we learn from these stories, do you think?

The Little Mermaid

Before you read

5 This story is about a *mermaid* and a *prince*. What are these words in your language? What do you think will happen in the story?

6 Are these sentences right or wrong? Find the words in *italics* in your dictionary.

    a Sport is usually good for your *body*.

    b People *kiss* their children.

    c Ships move on *land*.

    d *Magic* can change things.

    e *Plants* are usually green.

    f You cannot see a person's *soul*.

    g It hurts when you *touch* a very hot plate.

After you read

  7 How is magic important in this story?

  8 Work with another student.

    Student A: You are the little mermaid. You want to go on the land and be with your prince. Tell your sister.

    Student B: You are the little mermaid's sister. What does your sister really want? Will she be happy? Listen to her and then talk about the future with her.

The Emperor's New Clothes and Thumbelina

Before you read

  9 Look at the pictures on pages 25 and 28. What are these stories about, do you think?

10 Answer these questions about the words in italics.

    a Do we make cars from *cloth*?

    b Is an *emperor* an important man?

After you read

11 You are the emperor. Your servants catch the two men. What will you say to them?

12 You are the mole. How do you feel about Thumbelina now? Why?

Writing

13 Which story do you like best? Why? Write about the story and the people or animals in it.

14 You are the emperor. Write a letter to your sister in another country. Tell her the story of your clothes. What happened? How did you feel?

15 You are the 'ugly duckling' *or* Thumbelina *or* the king. It is one year later. Write about a day in your life.

16 Tell a tale from your own country.